PIANO • VOCAL • GUITAR

best of the PRETENDERS

Cover photo: Fin Costello/Redferns

ISBN 13: 978-1-4234-2110-8
ISBN 10: 1-4234-2110-8

HAL•LEONARD® CORPORATION
7777 W. BLUEMOUND RD. P.O. BOX 13819 MILWAUKEE, WI 53213

Visit Hal Leonard Online at
www.halleonard.com

contents

BACK ON THE CHAIN GANG 4

BRASS IN POCKET 12

DON'T GET ME WRONG 16

HUMAN ON THE INSIDE 23

HYMN TO HER 30

I GO TO SLEEP 38

I'LL STAND BY YOU 33

KID 42

MESSAGE OF LOVE 52

MIDDLE OF THE ROAD 58

MY CITY WAS GONE 47

MYSTERY ACHIEVEMENT 68

SENSE OF PURPOSE 74

STOP YOUR SOBBING 81

TALK OF THE TOWN 90

2000 MILES 86

BACK ON THE CHAIN GANG

Words and Music by
CHRISSIE HYNDE

BRASS IN POCKET

Words and Music by CHRISSIE HYNDE
and JAMES HONEYMAN-SCOTT

Moderate Rock

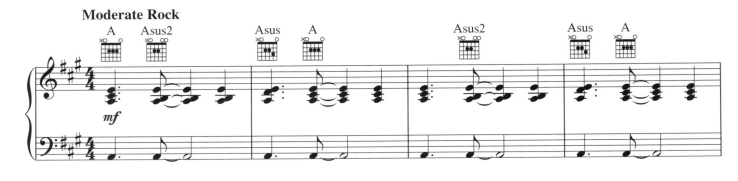

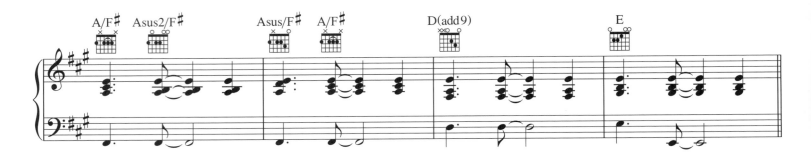

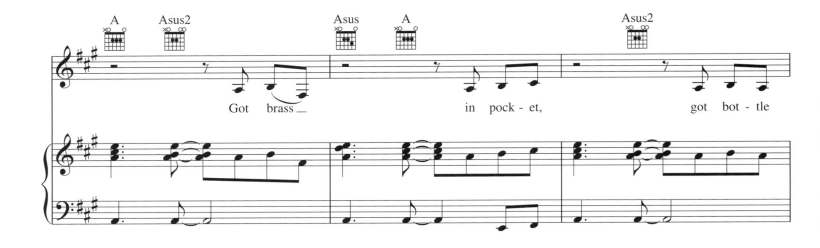

Got brass ___ in pock - et, got bot - tle

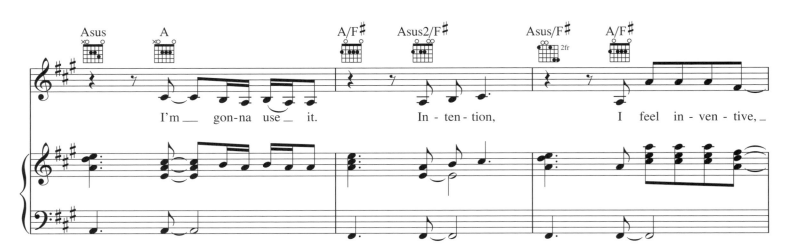

I'm ___ gon - na use ___ it.   In - ten - tion,   I feel in - ven - tive, ___

DON'T GET ME WRONG

Words and Music by
CHRISSIE HYNDE

Don't get me ___
Don't get me ___

Don't   get   me ___

HUMAN ON THE INSIDE

Words and Music by MARK McENTEE
and SHELLY PEIKEN

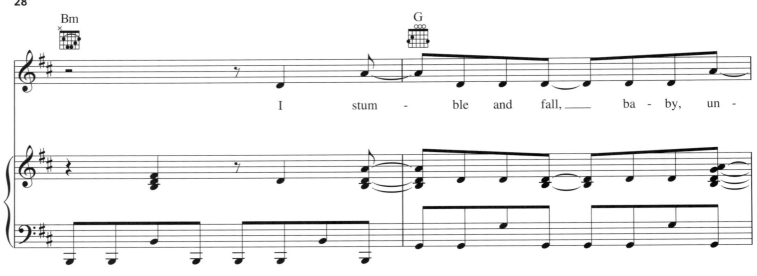

I stum - ble and fall, _____ ba - by, un -

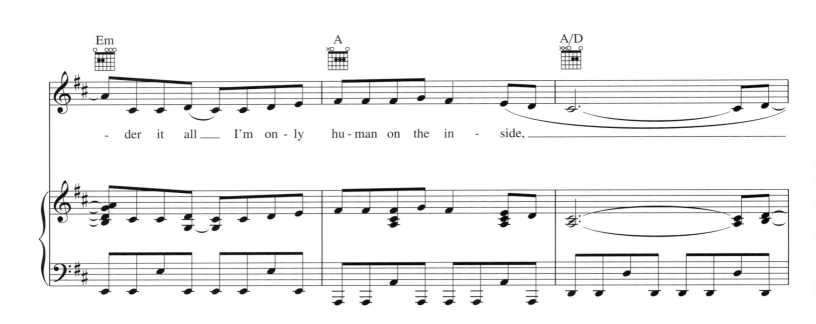

- der it all _____ I'm on - ly hu - man on the in - side, _____

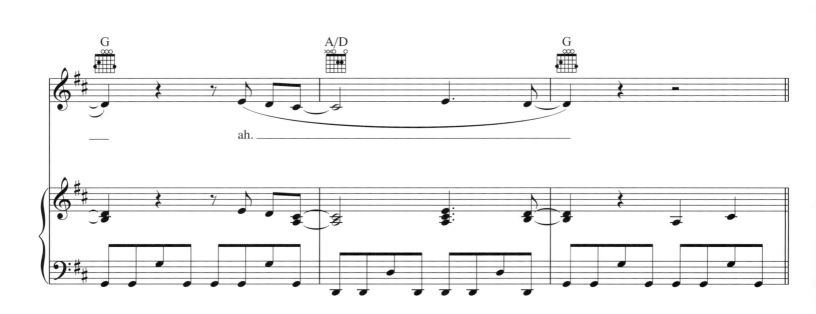

_____ ah. _____

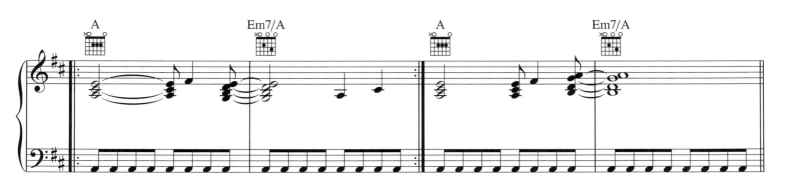

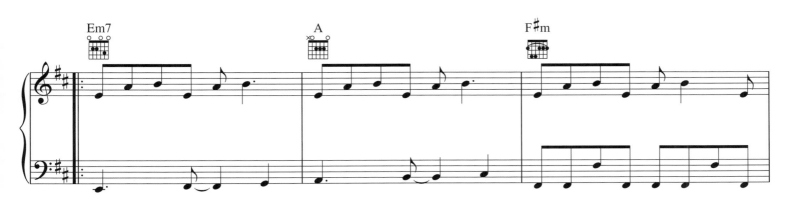

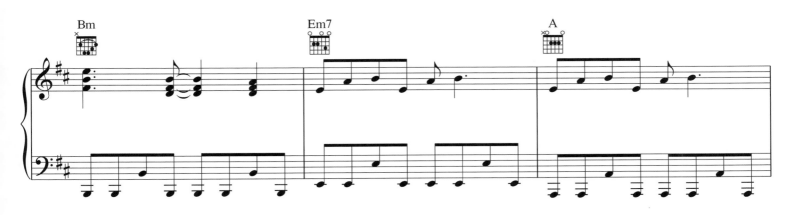

HYMN TO HER

Words and Music by
MEG KEENE

I'LL STAND BY YOU

Words and Music by CHRISSIE HYNDE,
TOM KELLY and BILLY STEINBERG

I GO TO SLEEP

Words and Music by
RAY DAVIES

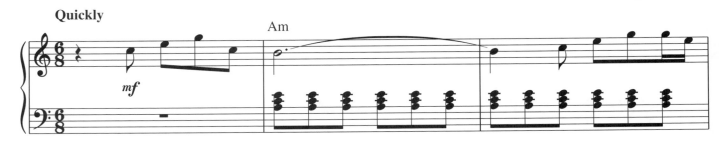

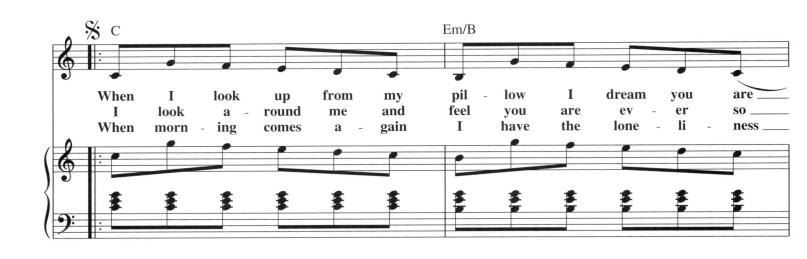

When I look up from my pil-low I dream you are
I look a-round from me and feel you are ev-er so ___
When morn-ing comes a-gain I have the lone-li-ness ___

___ there with me.
___ close to me.
___ you left me.

Though you are far a-way
Each tear that flows from my
Each day drags by un-til

To Coda

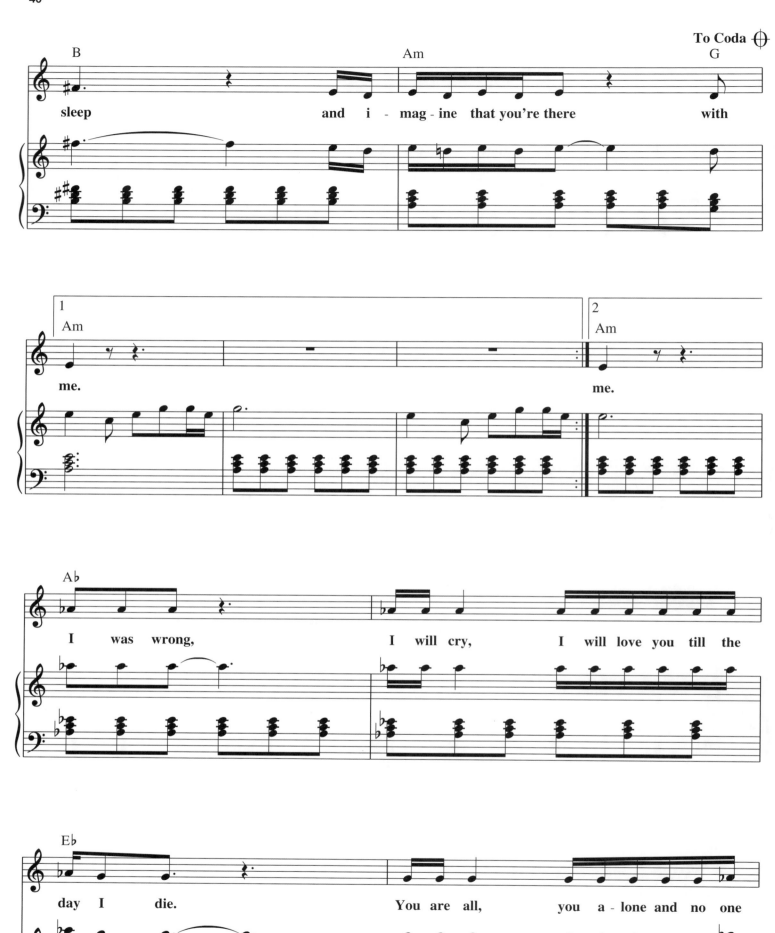

KID

Words and Music by
CHRISSIE HYNDE

MY CITY WAS GONE

Words and Music by
CHRISSIE HYNDE

MESSAGE OF LOVE

Words and Music by
CHRISSIE HYNDE

CODA

Say, "I love you, I love you, I love you, I love you, I love you, I love you.

Talk _ to me, dar - ling. Talk _ to me, dar - ling.

Repeat and Fade

MIDDLE OF THE ROAD

Words and Music by
CHRISSIE HYNDE

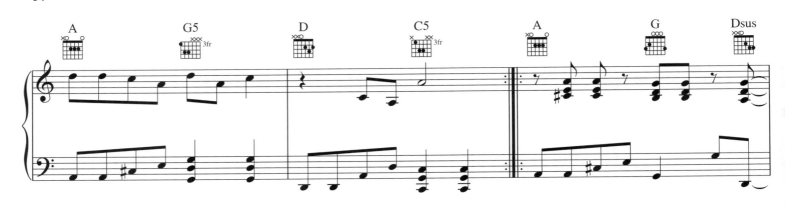

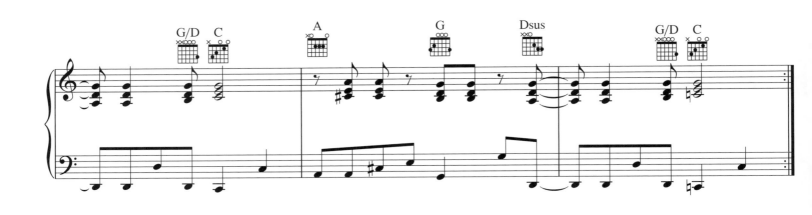

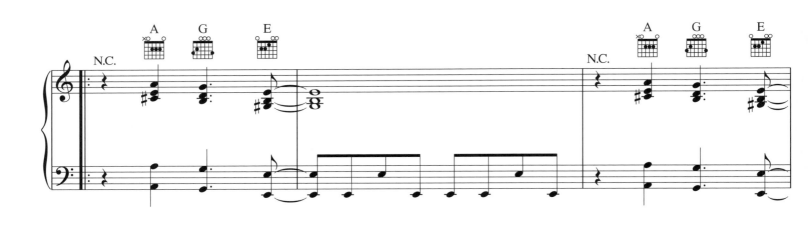

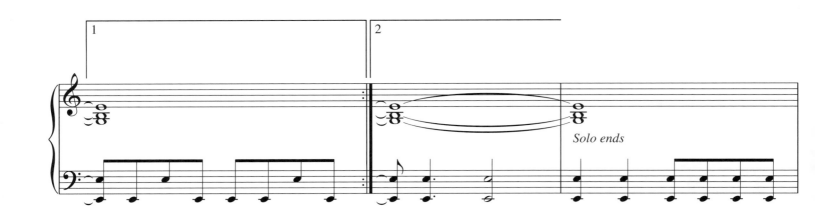

Come on, now, ___ in the mid - dle of the road, yeah.

Instrumental solo ad. lib

Play 3 times

MYSTERY ACHIEVEMENT

Words and Music by
CHRISSIE HYNDE

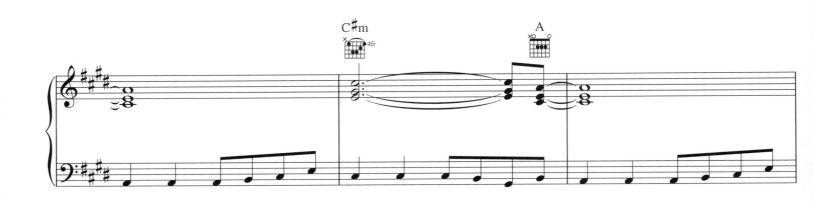

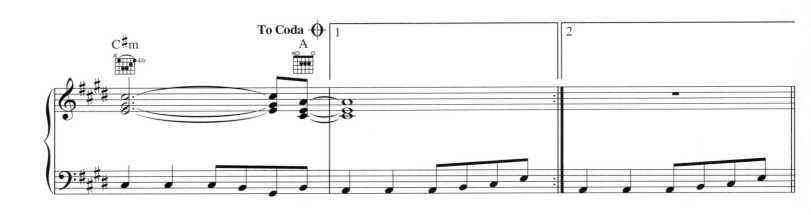

SENSE OF PURPOSE

Words and Music by
CHRISSIE HYNDE

Ev-ery-bod-y chokes when they see some-one cut down in their prime,
Bul-ly boys don't both-er me. I purse my lips and they run a-way,

STOP YOUR SOBBING

Words and Music by
RAY DAVIES

Moderate Rock

It is time ___ for you to stop ___ all of your sob - bing;

yes, it's time ___ for you to stop ___ all of this sob -

- bing, oh ___ oh. ___ There's one thing you got - ta do ___

2000 MILES

Words and Music by
CHRISSIE HYNDE

TALK OF THE TOWN

Words and Music by
CHRISSIE HYNDE

1. It's such a drag _____ to want some-thing some-
2. _____ to know what you feel _____

3. (See additional lyrics)

Additional Lyrics

3. Ah, but it's hard to live by the rules,
   I never could and still never do.
   But the rules and such never bothered you -
   You call the shots and they follow.
   I watch you still from a distance, then go
   back to my room - you'll never know.
   I want you - I want you but now -
   Who's the talk of the town?
   Chorus